Places
of
Poetry

A. F. Stewart

Places of Poetry
A. F. Stewart

Cover design by A. F. Stewart
Original artwork licensed by Adobe Stock Photos

ISBN: 978-1-9990659-3-5

More Books by A. F. Stewart

Poetry:

Horror Haiku Pas de Deux
Horror Haiku and Other Poems
Colours of Poetry
Reflections of Poetry
Shadows of Poetry
Tears of Poetry

Multi-Author Anthologies:

Hell's Empire: Tales of the Incursion
Abandon: 13 Tales of Impulse, Betrayal, Surrender, and Withdrawal
A Twist of Fate: A Collection of 11 Twisted Fairy Tales
Beyond the Wail
Legends and Lore
Mechanized Masterpieces
Christmas Lites Series (Books III-VII)
Coffin Hop: Death by Drive-In

Fiction:

Ghosts of the Sea Moon (Saga of the Outer Islands Book I)
Souls of the Dark Sea (Saga of the Outer Islands Book II)
Renegades of the Lost Sea (Saga of the Outer Islands Book III)
Chronicles of the Undead
Killers and Demons II: They Return
Killers and Demons
Fairy Tale Fusion
Gothic Cavalcade
Ruined City

Contents

Cities

Reciting by Moonlight

Quietly sitting in a Parisian café
beneath the night of a silver moon
not far from the Champs-Élysées

A peaceful, tranquil end of day
under starlit shafts from *la Lune*
quietly sitting in a Parisian café

Strains of Tennyson drift my way
as I stir espresso with a spoon
not far from the Champs-Élysées

Strong words, the voice holds sway
the impromptu recital, such a boon
quietly sitting in a Parisian café

I close my eyes, all cares away
in poetry immersed, ears attune
not far from the Champs-Élysées

A perfect night, coffee, a beignet
But alas this will end, far too soon
Quietly sitting in a Parisian café
not far from the Champs-Élysées

In Memory of Forgotten Loves

Wandering the streets of old Paris, lost
in tender thought, our woven dreams rose-glossed
Our sweet hands entangled, in youth's concord
grasping absolute love, as we adored,
until affection fled with winter's frost

Another love, passion's kiss breathed star-crossed
Fire and ice, lovers sailing tempest tossed
The flame died quickly; we became unmoored—
wandering the streets

Years produced caution, and love less embossed
reflected esteem, contemplated cost
I tried, but often her heart, I ignored
The day she left, I watched as the rain poured,
churning the soot and the smell of exhaust
wandering the streets

City of Lights

Against a sunset cerise
the lights of the city glow
A tapestry of time, a frieze
a glimmer in the river flow

The lights of the city glow
each one, a lovely spark;
a glimmer in the river flow
reflections in the dark

Each one, a lovely spark,
a tapestry of time, a frieze
Reflections in the dark,
against a sunset cerise

Cityscape

Set the scene against the amber streetlights...

Paris green swirls below
a teaspoon in the tinted glass
While the Moulin Rouge
beckons in scarlet petticoats

Change the view with the bright, cerise morning...

Riding the smoky blue river,
floating past a tangerine sun
against charcoal shadows
and titian summer reflections

Join the crowds as the day winds down to grey...

White haze and black trains calling,
the pulsing life veins of the city
Ruddy smudges and shaded stations
await the indistinguishable human hues.

The Poet

A tiny garret overlooking history
and candlelight against the moon
Scratched ink over new parchment
as lovers swoon on the riverside

He sees them from his window
or, perhaps, only in his thoughts
a mind's-eye illusion of amour
in the place that he calls home

Life

A sturdy bicycle, waiting
against the wrought-iron fence,
the early morning abating
A sturdy bicycle, waiting
Over coffee and croissants, debating
inconsequential offense
A sturdy bicycle, waiting
against the wrought-iron fence

Languishing in London

Pitter-patter comes the rain
across the river Thames
The double-decker honks its horn

To the pub and back again
Sometimes I want to scream
Pitter-patter comes the rain

Never much on the telly
I wish that I could soar
across the river Thames

My grey skies, my grey life
I step out into the street
The double-decker honks its horn

Roman Ruin

Ghosts of rose-coloured history,
weave Caligula in twilight silhouette
against the rumbling chariot's echo
and the soft-focus film of yesteryear
Cracked remains become Bread and Circuses
while the teeming Colosseum crowds cheer
Ghosts of rose-coloured history,
create an empire in perpetual illusion

Majestic Empire

From the ashes of old,
a republic slain
in blood and hubris
to rise anew
on columns of marble

Yet, in the shadows
of remnants, haunting
the foundation of ambition
cracked the stone
with an overreaching conceit

Unconquered Sun

Languid heat
of Barcelona
Where I dream
of fortunes
lost, hardship never vanquished
life's ashes scattered

City State

Intrigue under politics
in the city built of glass
Fortune's favour shifts
with the ever-changing tide,
gliding the canals of power
And blushing sunsets hide
the whispers in the night

Venetian Shadow

The darkened city bathed in a moonlit glow
lamplight casting reflections on the water cold
while the silence shrouded secrets hide below

Along the hushed avenue canals, row past row
come haunting whispers and mysteries unfold
The darkened city bathed in a moonlit glow

Exhumed from that lingering, forgotten undertow
hear the long echo of death from ages old
while the silence shrouded secrets hide below

Intrigues, politics, favours to bestow
Commerce and war, and betrayal bold
The darkened city bathed in a moonlit glow

Scattered pieces toppled like a fallen domino
all commoners and kings to be bought and sold
while the silence shrouded secrets hide below

Shattered glass in a ghostly silhouette allegro
murky truth shifting transverse of a threshold
The darkened city bathed in a moonlit glow
while the silence shrouded secrets hide below

In Bruges

A slice of time frozen
in stone, along the canals
Flemish spires reaching
ever towards an open sky,
a belfry tower standing guard
Hear the echoes of eras past
along the cobblestone lanes

An Evening in Amsterdam

A warm orange glow, reflected in blue,
the canal smooth and still as glass
Beauty sublime, bid the day adieu
A warm orange glow, reflected in blue
Stand in the calm, soak in the view
amid the boats, bicycles, and brass
A warm orange glow, reflected in blue,
the canal smooth and still as glass

At the Gate

Beneath antiquity's shadow
walking with the ghosts
of a blood-soaked yesteryear

History
Victory
Majesty
Society

Defiance
Against exponential revolution

Triumph and Procession
At the Gate

Berlin Cabaret

Cigarette smoke and the dim light
the stock crowd on a rainy night
From the stage, some soft jazz
and a singer in the limelight
Music pure, sweet notes; nothing trite
No glitzy razzmatazz

Blooms in the City

Sidewalk crack peeking
up. A little green shoot
turned to the sunlight
reflection in glass
skyscrapers

Warm spring air
blowing. Growing tall
against the bustle,
hustle of every
passerby.

Velvet petals stretching
free. A splash of colour
standing in the grey,
thriving in the concrete
jungle

Shadows in the Rain

Thrumming droplets
a firm, cascading deluge beat
Thrumming droplets
cast from sky borne water faucets,
turned on to drown the latent heat
Black reflection shapes coat the street
Thrumming droplets

Lilac Cadillac

Violet light reflecting on the chrome
The flashy neon lighting up the night
Strains of jazz and a little R&B
From would-be stars eager to play
Laughter and beer, and cigarette smoke
A packed house, a late night,
Welcome to the hottest club in town.

Rural

Heartland

Twilight Blues

Come 'round, come 'round
when the sun sets down
and the moon rises to play
When we strum the guitar,
and they roll up from afar
to hear twilight blues on the bay

We wail at the night,
get all the notes right;
our midnight music soiree
It's fiddle and bass,
the harmony we chase
to hear twilight blues on the bay

Maestro

Echo of the Spanish sun
streaked on canvas
as the faint rhythms
of music play against
laughter and aroma
The scent of paella drifts
on the dry summer wind
while the church bells
wait to chime
The open window shines
the perfect light
and the last brushstroke
splays with colour

Mountain Sanctuary

Serenity,
a quiet corner tucked away
Serenity
Rediscovering sanity
watching the sunrise greet each day
isolation breathing past grey
Serenity

Picturesque

Like fire on the mountain snow
nestled in the quiet night;
splendid in a silhouette glow

Sheltered from the chill wind flow,
a stark, beautiful, enduring sight
Like fire on the mountain snow

High above the world below,
a lustrous view, a beacon bright
Splendid in a silhouette glow

Shimmering wonder to bestow
enchantment, from a height
Like fire on the mountain snow

Gleaming clear, a midnight hello
to stir ideal dreams to flight
Splendid in a silhouette glow

Moment in time, a flawless show,
a perfect picturesque delight
Like fire on the mountain snow,
splendid in a silhouette glow

Black Wings and a Feather

A lofty corner of the world
touching the sky and the black wings
of circling ravens

A feather falls into the chasm
a dark speck descending the current
past the clouds

Silence

Still water, morning
the calm lake—serenity
the loon calls to me

Whispers in the Wind

Lay your head down
in the prairie meadows
while the stars drift overhead
Close your tired eyes
against your burdens,
your breath calm and even
Let the wind caress your face
and soothe your cares
Let the wind whisper your name

Travelling

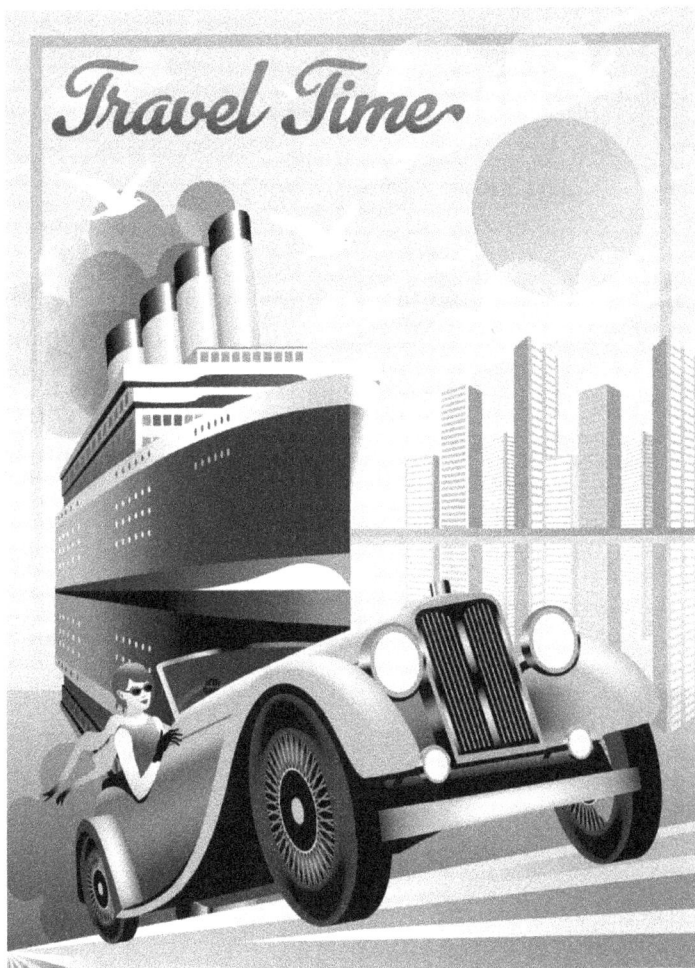

Passengers

Steel-encased community ready for an airplane odyssey
soaring from gravity, yet... only another mundane odyssey

Noise and crowds, dour faces waiting for the next departure
packed like sardines, embarking on their daily train odyssey

Far from the Aegean, bobbing on the sea like a crumbling cork
pleasure cruising, seeking existential solace on a vain odyssey

Asphalt beneath rubber, chattering children in the back seat
wishing you could run from your life; a changing lane odyssey

Caught on the riptide of circumstance and expected choices
fitting in, wearing out, another passenger on the pain odyssey

Getting There

Tread
apace
across worlds,
stars as your guide
There and back again,
chant the wanderers creed
to speed a nimble journey
Adventure awaits, for the bold
The road to the horizon beckons,
calls to your nomadic heart with a song

Elsewhere Dawn

Wafts a sultry breeze,
born of the jasmine wind
through the timeworn streets
Scents of cinnamon and cardamom,
fresh baking bread and salty skin,
salute the aurora daybreak
Gossamer illumination sways,
folding gilded light into zephyr

Far From Home

Across the sea I've wandered deep
I raced away from hills and sheep
Now in this hour along
rise memories I dared to keep,
and tears I thought I'd never weep
wrapped in a highland song

Sights Unseen

A photograph,
a little dusty, a little faded,
of a city far away
Someone's dream
of youth, of promises unkept,
lost in transitory years
That glamorous metropolis
abandoned, but not forgotten

The Stars and Moon

Crossroad In Time

starlight across matter
and pin drop particles
eons smashed together

one breath, one step
zigzag right, allemande left
starlight across matter

fragility, fluidity, origins
complex might-have-been
and pin drop particles

constructed existence
perpetually balancing
eons smashed together

Star Struck

Stare into the galactic night,
yawning canopy of pinprick light
Reach up, reach up...

embrace conflagration
soar your imagination
system-wide nullification
of planetary gravitation
a temporary aberration,
when you can touch the stars

Boundary

Against moon and stars, infinity breaks
in ripples of cosmic shattered dust
indigo beams of world-stuff lost
a violet edge of ruin
between negated void
and freed creation
caught in the tide,
whirlwind storm
of vast
space

Transitions

Shift position
Across luminosity stars
Shift position
Great transitory ambition
Set down in galactic memoirs
galloping past Venus and Mars
Shift position

Towards the Moon

The breath of Endymion
sails towards the moon,
on a silver sea of stars
around the night ethereal
Past dreams and realms
in the hoary wake of gods
Blown along the cosmic nexus
towards home.

Welcome Moon

The waltzing night brings jasmine
a perfume caress to herald sighs,
the breath of breeze amongst the trees
that spreads to trace the stars
Quiet footsteps linger
between the grasses strewn
Eyes that glitter to the sky,
Oh, welcome moon

A stroll about the garden
when souls do chase their sleep
plucks the strings of ecstasy
and banishes the cares
Of wonders great, and solitude,
a smile, a dance, a snatch of tune
'Tis a night to be alive
underneath the blessed moon

Memories from imaginings
tangle in the vines
and perch upon closed petals
as the roses slumber well
Stillness follows pace and turn
with nature's bounty to commune
Such an eve for remembrance
Shine, oh light of the moon

If only one could stay the course
Here amid the sweet nocturne
Yet it shall not be but a brief respite,

a momentary dalliance
Drink in the wind, the stars, the night,
for serenity, it ends too soon
With a tear, and a whisper,
and a farewell moon

Can You See The Moon?

Can you see the moon, under its mosaic glass?
Far above a gossamer turtle in the turquoise sea,
blowing bubble kisses to a sun bleached corsage.

Imprinted moments, captured points of light
Smeared concurrently, primary colours of display
Can you see the moon, under its mosaic glass?

Mellow ripples, flowing, ebbing, now and then
filtered prisms and perceptions dancing on a pin,
far above a gossamer turtle in the turquoise sea.

Wave hello, wave goodbye, spinning turntable
Music plays, evermore, nevermore, while you're
blowing bubble kisses to a sun bleached corsage.

Beyond the Blue Moon

Beyond the pale moon, blue
flies a stardust dream so true
Past the universe's morning dew,
beyond the pale moon, blue
To expanse and time it bids adieu,
transcending wonders, stars anew
Beyond the pale moon, blue
flies a stardust dream so true

Woodland Moon

The silver moon in an obsidian sky,
its light caught in the canopy of trees,
while leaves flutter against a sigh
The silver moon in an obsidian sky
Sometimes it hides as clouds float by
a coquette, a dance, a celestial tease
The silver moon in an obsidian sky,
its light caught in the canopy of trees

The Sea

The Sea, A Ship, A Star

A guiding star, is what I ask
within the sky of blackened night
Above the windblown sails,
that glitter beacon homeward

Fifty Fathoms Deep

Stygian squelch and salty brine
where the carrion fall to slumber
Inky black and a wet drowned hell
with the monsters coloured umber
It's where I live
Fifty fathoms deep

The raven grave and eternal abyss
for ships that sunk from battle
flesh picked clean and washed away
Nothing left but a dead bone rattle
It's where I live
Fifty fathoms deep

It's submerged tears of last regrets
in the face of your abandoned faith
Whispers and screams come empty
in the home of the devil's wraith
It's where I died,
and rose again
Fifty fathoms deep

Sailor's Voyage

In the stormy seas, come clouds or rain,
with swaying ship, firm footing upon the deck,
the whitecapped waves hearken home
Busy sailors smile, watching daylight dim;
shining stars appear above
Ocean's composed calm, that hazy hour
of peerless paradise, of brief bliss

Song of the Siren

Voices weaving their harmonic illusions
along the undulating waves of the sea
Forever beckoning sailors' delusions

Come to us, sail the wind, leave your cares, be free
We welcome you, accept you, you will be home
Bask in the warm sun, under a cypress tree

The sultry song drifting across ocean foam,
their sweet persuasion and promises untrue
cast to wind and fate, wherever sailors roam

For you sailors bold, beyond the waters blue
We offer paradise, start your life anew

Still Sea

In the star-kissed arms of the night,
against the soft melody of the waves,
you stand on deck, seeing the beyond
Past the horizon, across the ocean
to the worlds untouched, shimmers
in the waiting sunrise
In the star-kissed arms of the night,
against the soft melody of the waves
Where the surface reflects like dark glass
into your soul

Sand, Shells, and Sea

In the early morning I am here. Hear
the surf against the sand. And
smile with sunlight in my eye. I
wiggle my toes against the wet. Wet
sea lapping over shells. Shells
echoing the ocean blue. Blew
my cares out to sea. See
the morning dawn. Dawn.

Stand on Shore

Stand on shore
while the fishermen sail
Wave goodbye
Pray for calm
and not for storm
to see your men at the end of the day

Stand on shore
as the sailors leave
Wipe your tears
about promises made
and tell your lies
that he'll return to you one day

Stand on shore
while sons sail to war
Hold back tears
with silent prayers
as your heart stands frozen
in fragile hope of reunion some day

Other Realms

BEYOND
WORLDS

Soul's Revelry

Past the knoll,
music soothes a yearning soul
Bring your mirth, and wine to sup
Raise your cup and fill your bowl

Glimpse the Fae,
come to dance the gloaming grey
Join the step, be swept along
Heed the song, do come and play

Dawn will toll,
remember not, time they stole
Their secrets kept, that's the rule
The price you'll give, past the knoll

Another Day, Another Life

Another day with grey clouds, pouring
or another life under sundrenched skies
Two souls falling through the universe

Misfortune into misery, cycled forward
until the dawn fades, and hope scalds
Another day with grey clouds, pouring

Cordial mornings, highlighted sanguine
sliding into carefree, a perfection dream
or another life under sundrenched skies

Side by side, yet eon particles apart
mirrored existence, parallel subsistence
Two souls falling through the universe

The Candle Remained Burning

In the window the candle remained burning,
that frail, solitary light lingering in the world
A beacon against the dark, a last hope yearning,
flickering flame with wisps of smoke curled

That frail, solitary light lingering in the world
nestled near a frosted pane, shining in the night,
flickering flame with wisps of smoke curled
gently calling the lost from their desperate flight

Nestled near a frosted pane, shining in the night
Ignited long days past by an anonymous hand,
gently calling the lost from their desperate flight
to a wayside respite, far afield from their homeland

Ignited long days past by an anonymous hand,
a beacon against the dark, a last hope yearning.
To a wayside respite, far afield from their homeland;
in the window the candle remained burning

Seraphim Woods

Beyond the dark, in the faraway worlds,
past the wispy zephyrs of a lost horizon
the whippoorwill calls, and the raven sings
of death and pain, and the shadows sharp
Keep to the path, don't stray a step
Don't walk alone in Seraphim Woods

Beyond the twilight, in the murky mists
moonlight nocturnal will waltz with the dead
while ancient rhymes disturb mortal sanity
and lullabies croon to forgotten beasts
Keep to the path, don't stray a step
Don't walk alone in Seraphim Woods.

Beyond the realms, where the ravening dwell,
where the footsteps crackle on the empty wind,
and the trees shiver as strange creatures pass,
their muted voices whispering furtive names
Keep to the path, don't stray a step
Don't walk alone in Seraphim Woods.

The Red Queens

Rivers flow in crimson streams
with blood a thousand-fold
and tears of the blackened damned
Seared demon mists
roil from the wormy earth
blown on brimstone winds

Can you hear them call?
Can you hear them laugh?
The Red Queens walk tonight

Spirits claw from beneath their graves,
born again with baneful verve
from cracking bones and rancid flesh
And while they howl their spite
toward this forlorn night,
they scurry to heed the summons

Can you hear them call?
Can you hear them shriek?
The Red Queens walk tonight

The Red Queens stalk the night

Magic Lost

Once, among the mists,
and wisps of summer breeze
the sylvan elves ruled,
the capricious faeries roamed

Once, beneath the earth
in the caves, amid the stone,
the dwarves mined their gold
and the hungry dragons slept

The Stone Road

Mist rolls across the meadow
while the deep shadow grows
and the bitter wind blows
Down the long stone road

Not a living soul to be seen
Yet, hear the faint footfalls
as the taciturn bird calls
Down the long stone road

Shall the bloodstains manifest?
Do the drumbeats echo high,
that last, heralding cry?
Down the long stone road

Or do whispers walk the dead,
our memories let loose
from the shattered truce
Down the long stone road

Just slipshod miles to trudge,
with distant promises to keep
and forgotten debts to reap
Down the long stone road

Kingsbrook Lane

The wind blows bitter
in among the hollows
Down and deep
where the black shadow follows
On Kingsbrook Lane

Whispers chase the twilight
past faded rosewood hedge
round and round
calling from civility's edge
On Kingsbrook Lane

With the hoary moonbeams
dancing in the night
Debts come due
and no one hears the screams
On Kingsbrook Lane

Unsettled Places

Light in the Window

Against the glass, the smallest glimmer
a wayward shine within the night
A lone beacon, that solitary sprite
Against the glass, the smallest glimmer

A wayward shine within the night,
perhaps a flicker of what used to be
now adrift, discarded, a forlorn plea
A wayward shine within the night

Perhaps a flicker of what used to be
Oh, those halcyon days of lively mirth
days of love, of contentment, of worth
Perhaps a flicker of what used to be

Oh, those halcyon days of lively mirth,
against the glass, the smallest glimmer
Maybe a memory, a recollected shimmer
Oh, those halcyon days of lively mirth,

Against the glass, the smallest glimmer
a wayward shine within the night
A lone beacon, that solitary sprite
Against the glass, the smallest glimmer

Glass Bottles

She places them on the window ledge,
in a row
against the red curtain faded by the sun
hollow glass
remnants of her past, and others she never knew
a comfort
A hint of who she was, her dusty days of glory
long ended

The Back Garden

Standing in the doorway
to the back porch
The apple tree
shades the garden
and the cat stalks the birds
You listen for the voices
out of habit,
children's laughter
so far away now
But memories comfort you
standing in the doorway

Morning Lilies

Sunlight through the grey clouds
scattering light across the shadows
of the neglected garden.
White lilies in an unkempt bed,
overgrown green, beneath soft petals.
She still sits and smiles
with a lingering gaze, admiring the flowers
while she sips her tea on a balmy morning.
She never looks at the empty chair beside her.

Once Upon a Time

Faded flower patterns
on outdated wallpaper;
fashionable in its time
The pianoforte
is out of tune,
but she plays
a melancholy melody
to the empty room
It echoes distant years
and breaking memories
Their forgotten faces
and jumbled names
impressions in the air

As Petals Fall

As petals fall in rain
cerise velvet from the sky
white-streaked and fragrant
I stare into the orchard
Tears reflecting the weather
Remembering

Serenade In G

The faint scent of rosin in a quiet room
the polished wood against fingertips
Closed eyes and a lifted bow
to make the violin sing

To sing of heartbreak on a winter's morn
of lovers past, along the riverside
of the café and coffee, and their laughter

It sings of jealousy and mistrust
of fights and tears and making up
of nights staring at the stars, entwined

It sings their heartbeat,
It plays their joy
It is the melody of love

Beyond

Outside the existential
waits unfathomable
indistinguishable
from the mundane
philosophy
smashing past
chaotic images
until authenticity
becomes delusion
and aberration
shifts reality

Ferry Ride

One coin for a passage
laid against the tongue
in the silence of mourning

The rhythm of the dirge,
an echo of the River Styx
One coin for a passage

A glint of silver in the sun
payment for the ferryman
laid against the tongue

Honouring rite and ritual
while the living move onward
in the silence of mourning

Lost Son

The bleak north wind
across the lonely field,
rippling the violet heather
as bagpipes lament their tune

The mournful undertones
shed the rising dawn
along the lonely fields
of silent tragedy.

Voices from the Grave

I stand, the wind at my back,
the creaking cemetery gate open;
they beckon me, the dead
The ones I've lost
I can smell the damp earth,
still wet from morning dew
I hear the whispered names
of my family

The wind carries their murmurs
My voices from the grave

Abandoned

Salient reverberations
into crumbling structure
overgrown in ruin and moss
Rusty metal doors
hang askew in silhouette
their broken hinges creaking
in the cold autumn wind

Pete Was Here

Pete was here?
Pete is where?
Where in the world?
Where did he go?
Go past forever
Go 'til you drop
Drop in
Drop out
Out of time
Out in the universe
Universe surrounds
Universe confounds
Confounds existence
Confounds persistence
Persistence anonymity
Persistence quality
Quality for your dollar
Quality control
Control on a budget
Control freak
Freak chic
Freak passé
Passé dancing
Passé disallowed
Disallowed engagement
Disallowed reflection
Reflection in the mirror
Reflection sympathy
Sympathy sonata
Sympathy for the devil

Devil dog
Devil you know
Know what?
Know when?
When is the question
When did he leave?
Leave today
Leave forever
Forever descending
Forever in a moment
Moment consumed
Moment resumed
Resumed mentality
Resumed the search
Search wide
Search infinity
Infinity of Pete
Infinity found
Found
Pete

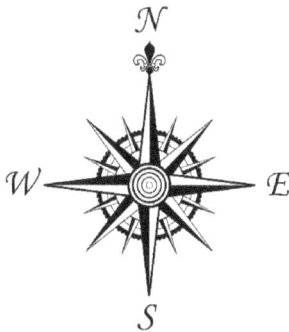

cracked
dreams bright
summer
Empire
Haiku
light Saga
always
Paris
sturdy
bathed
Elysees
ghosts
City
bicycle coffee
Islands
eyes
calm
history
mountain
silence
silhouette
secrets
Tales
bitter
Champs
reflections
tapestry potter
music
night
hear
blue
City
city
flow
across
hide day glass
reflected Stewart
love snow
along shadows
morning twilight
stone green
blood
shrouded moonlit
darkened
Fairy Bells
drift strains
grey still
hook
fire
sitting
perfect
streets river far
eternity splendid
play street
glow
Poetry
time
moon
coming
echo
wind
writing
cerise
come
droplets
Parisian
yester year
darker

A steadfast and proud sci-fi and fantasy geek, A. F. Stewart was born and raised in Nova Scotia, Canada and still calls it home. The youngest in a family of seven children, she always had an overly creative mind and an active imagination. She favours the dark and deadly when writing—her genres of choice being dark fantasy and horror—but she has been known to venture into the light on occasion. As an indie author she's published novels, novellas and story collections, with a few side trips into poetry.